GRATITUDE

Create a more positive life with gratitude

GRATITUDE

Create a more positive life with gratitude

© 2016 Claus Skærlund-Dall

Publisher: BoD – Books on Demand Copenhagen, Denmark
Manufacture BoD – Books on Demand GmbH Norderstedt, Germany

ISBN: 978-1542626538

Introdution

This book is for those who want to add more focus on the positive things that happen in your life by focusing more on gratitude.

While gratitude is used in religious connections, it can be so much more.

If I look on gratitude through my eyes as a life coach, I see a fantastic tool for focusing on the good and positive things that happen every day in our lives. Scientific studies show that having focus on gratitude for 7 days, will have an effect for up to 3 month after.

When you start filling out this book, will it mean that you never will think about the negative things? No, but we will get our subconscious to have more focus on the positive things.

If you have had a tendency to have focus on the negative, it can be difficult in the beginning to find somethings to be grateful for. If this is the case for you, then just start with small things. They are just as important as the big things, if not more important.

An example on this could be:

- I'm grateful for the sun is shining today.

- I'm grateful that I slept all night without waking up.

- I'm grateful that I only took one small piece of cake today.

When we make it a habit, we slowly get better to put words on the things we are grateful for. There is no right or wrong way to do it, there is only your way.

Personally, I always use the bottom part of the page to write, what I will do to make the day better and more positive. If you write in the book in the evening you can write what you will do for the next day.

An example on this could be:

- Today, I will hold the door for people I meet.

- Today, I will smile to people I come in contact with.

- Today, I will give my wife a big hug and kiss when I come home.

Write whatever will get you in a good mood.

If there are days where you miss writing in the book, and there will be. Then take responsibility for this and write *"today I decided to skip writing"*. That way you can take responsibility for skipping and gradually take responsibility of your life and actions. This is a good alternative from getting irritated and blaming others for it.

In this, you are not allowed to write negative things! This is not a traditional diary, where you can write your up and downs. This book is only for the positive thoughts in your life.

This will get your attention on all the good, lovely and fantastic things that happens in your life every day.

If you are nervous or afraid that you're not able to find something to write, then remember *"fear is only a part of your imagination about the future, it is not real"*

So jump in and have fantastic time writing.

Claus Skærlund-Dall
NLP master coach

Day: Date:

I am grateful for...

I am grateful for...

I am grateful for...

Today I will...

Day: Date:

I am grateful for...

I am grateful for...

I am grateful for...

Today I will...

Day: Date:

I am grateful for...

I am grateful for...

I am grateful for...

Today I will...

Day: Date:

I am grateful for...

I am grateful for...

I am grateful for...

Today I will...

4

Day: Date:

I am grateful for...

I am grateful for...

I am grateful for...

Today I will...

Day: Date:

I am grateful for...

I am grateful for...

I am grateful for...

Today I will...

6

Day: Date:

I am grateful for...

I am grateful for...

I am grateful for...

Today I will...

"Our brains don't differentiate fantasy and the real world.

For many years, I was very good at staying in a negative state, by letting my fantasy run free with discussion and situations that never had happened or never will happen.

But by having these fantasies, my body responded like it had happened and as a result, I kept having negative feelings in my body."

– Claus Skærlund-Dall

Day: Date:

I am grateful for...

I am grateful for...

I am grateful for...

Today I will...

Day: Date:

I am grateful for...

I am grateful for...

I am grateful for...

Today I will...

Day: Date:

I am grateful for...

I am grateful for...

I am grateful for...

Today I will...

Day: Date:

I am grateful for...

I am grateful for...

I am grateful for...

Today I will...

Day: Date:

I am grateful for...

I am grateful for...

I am grateful for...

Today I will...

Day: Date:

I am grateful for...

I am grateful for...

I am grateful for...

Today I will...

14

Day: Date:

I am grateful for...

I am grateful for...

I am grateful for...

Today I will...

GREAT!

You have reached day 15 with focus on all the good things in your life, you are grateful for."

Day: Date:

I am grateful for...

I am grateful for...

I am grateful for...

Today I will...

Day: Date:

I am grateful for...

I am grateful for...

I am grateful for...

Today I will...

Day: Date:

I am grateful for...

I am grateful for...

I am grateful for...

Today I will...

Day: Date:

I am grateful for...

I am grateful for...

I am grateful for...

Today I will...

20

Day: Date:

I am grateful for...

I am grateful for...

I am grateful for...

Today I will...

Day: Date:

I am grateful for...

I am grateful for...

I am grateful for...

Today I will...

22

Day: Date:

I am grateful for...

I am grateful for...

I am grateful for...

Today I will...

Have you thought about how you know you are happy, sad or afraid?

You can't have a feeling without it being a physical feeling in your body. It can be in your stomach, chest, jaw or even your shoulders.

My happy feeling is in the upper part of my stomach and it is a roaring red liquid.

When you have written your 3 things of gratitude, try to close your eyes and think of them. Now notice what happens in your body and where."

– Claus Skærlund-Dall

Day: Date:

I am grateful for...

I am grateful for...

I am grateful for...

Today I will...

Day: Date:

I am grateful for...

I am grateful for...

I am grateful for...

Today I will...

Day: Date:

I am grateful for...

I am grateful for...

I am grateful for...

Today I will...

Day: Date:

I am grateful for...

I am grateful for...

I am grateful for...

Today I will...

28

Day: Date:

I am grateful for...

I am grateful for...

I am grateful for...

Today I will...

Day: Date:

I am grateful for...

I am grateful for...

I am grateful for...

Today I will...

Day: Date:

I am grateful for...

I am grateful for...

I am grateful for...

Today I will...

"The best way to show my gratitude is to accept everything, even my problems with joy."

– *Mother Teresa*

Day: Date:

I am grateful for...

I am grateful for...

I am grateful for...

Today I will...

Day: Date:

I am grateful for...

I am grateful for...

I am grateful for...

Today I will...

Day: Date:

I am grateful for...

I am grateful for...

I am grateful for...

Today I will...

Day: Date:

I am grateful for...

I am grateful for...

I am grateful for...

Today I will...

Day: Date:

I am grateful for...

I am grateful for...

I am grateful for...

Today I will...

Day: Date:

I am grateful for...

I am grateful for...

I am grateful for...

Today I will...

Day: Date:

I am grateful for...

I am grateful for...

I am grateful for...

Today I will...

Remember to be grateful for the things that happen in your life and, the things you normally would consider as failure, defeat or mistakes.

Be grateful for these things and the experience they have given you."

– Claus Skærlund-Dall

Day: Date:

I am grateful for...

I am grateful for...

I am grateful for...

Today I will...

Day: Date:

I am grateful for...

I am grateful for...

I am grateful for...

Today I will...

Day: Date:

I am grateful for...

I am grateful for...

I am grateful for...

Today I will...

Day: Date:

I am grateful for...

I am grateful for...

I am grateful for...

Today I will...

Day: Date:

I am grateful for...

I am grateful for...

I am grateful for...

Today I will...

Day: Date:

I am grateful for...

I am grateful for...

I am grateful for...

Today I will...

Day: Date:

I am grateful for...

I am grateful for...

I am grateful for...

Today I will...

In my younger years, I was very shy and for many years I couldn't stand up in crowds and talk.

It got better as I got older, but it was first when I learned to how to model other people, by using NLP, I could do it without getting a stomach ache and feeling my voice quiver.

Someone I used to model is Bill Clinton, by using his body language and how I think this makes him feel.

Try to find a person you look up to or that does something you would like to do. Find out what their body language, tone, or thoughts are. Now model these things."

– Claus Skærlund-Dall

Day: Date:

I am grateful for...

I am grateful for...

I am grateful for...

Today I will...

Day: Date:

I am grateful for...

I am grateful for...

I am grateful for...

Today I will...

Day: Date:

I am grateful for...

I am grateful for...

I am grateful for...

Today I will...

Day: Date:

I am grateful for...

I am grateful for...

I am grateful for...

Today I will...

Day: Date:

I am grateful for...

I am grateful for...

I am grateful for...

Today I will...

Day: Date:

I am grateful for...

I am grateful for...

I am grateful for...

Today I will...

54

Day: Date:

I am grateful for...

I am grateful for...

I am grateful for...

Today I will...

"My life isn't perfect,
but I'm thankful
for everything I have."

Day: Date:

I am grateful for...

I am grateful for...

I am grateful for...

Today I will...

Day: Date:

I am grateful for...

I am grateful for...

I am grateful for...

Today I will...

58

Day: Date:

I am grateful for...

I am grateful for...

I am grateful for...

Today I will...

Day: Date:

I am grateful for...

I am grateful for...

I am grateful for...

Today I will...

Day: Date:

I am grateful for...

I am grateful for...

I am grateful for...

Today I will...

Day: Date:

I am grateful for...

I am grateful for...

I am grateful for...

Today I will...

Day: Date:

I am grateful for...

I am grateful for...

I am grateful for...

Today I will...

Our brains are so greatly made that it will create the connections we choose.

So if we have focus on the negative things for some time, the synapses in the brain will let go of the connection they use to have and create connections that now will make chemical connections that will increase the negative feeling in the body.

But by getting focus back to the positive things in your life, you will create these connections. again."

– *Claus Skærlund-Dall*

Day: Date:

I am grateful for...

I am grateful for...

I am grateful for...

Today I will...

Day: Date:

I am grateful for...

I am grateful for...

I am grateful for...

Today I will...

Day: Date:

I am grateful for...

I am grateful for...

I am grateful for...

Today I will...

Day: Date:

I am grateful for...

I am grateful for...

I am grateful for...

Today I will...

Day: Date:

I am grateful for...

I am grateful for...

I am grateful for...

Today I will...

Day: Date:

I am grateful for...

I am grateful for...

I am grateful for...

Today I will...

Day: Date:

I am grateful for...

I am grateful for...

I am grateful for...

Today I will...

"Gratitude turns what we have into enough."

– Melody Beattie

Day: Date:

I am grateful for...

I am grateful for...

I am grateful for...

Today I will...

Day: Date:

I am grateful for...

I am grateful for...

I am grateful for...

Today I will...

Day: Date:

I am grateful for...

I am grateful for...

I am grateful for...

Today I will...

Day: Date:

I am grateful for...

I am grateful for...

I am grateful for...

Today I will...

Day: Date:

I am grateful for...

I am grateful for...

I am grateful for...

Today I will...

Day: Date:

I am grateful for...

I am grateful for...

I am grateful for...

Today I will...

Day: Date:

I am grateful for...

I am grateful for...

I am grateful for...

Today I will...

F eeling gratitude and not expressing it
is like wrapping a present and not giving it."

– *William Arthur Ward*

Day: Date:

I am grateful for...

I am grateful for...

I am grateful for...

Today I will...

Day: Date:

I am grateful for...

I am grateful for...

I am grateful for...

Today I will...

Day: Date:

I am grateful for...

I am grateful for...

I am grateful for...

Today I will...

Day: Date:

I am grateful for...

I am grateful for...

I am grateful for...

Today I will...

Day: Date:

I am grateful for...

I am grateful for...

I am grateful for...

Today I will...

Day: Date:

I am grateful for...

I am grateful for...

I am grateful for...

Today I will...

Day: Date:

I am grateful for...

I am grateful for...

I am grateful for...

Today I will...

"Develop an attitude of gratitude, and give thanks for everything that happens to you, knowing that every step forward is a step toward achieving something bigger and better than your current situation."

– *Brian Tracy*

Day: Date:

I am grateful for...

I am grateful for...

I am grateful for...

Today I will...

Day: Date:

I am grateful for...

I am grateful for...

I am grateful for...

Today I will...

Day: Date:

I am grateful for...

I am grateful for...

I am grateful for...

Today I will...

Day: Date:

I am grateful for...

I am grateful for...

I am grateful for...

Today I will...

92

Day: Date:

I am grateful for...

I am grateful for...

I am grateful for...

Today I will...

Day: Date:

I am grateful for...

I am grateful for...

I am grateful for...

Today I will...

Day: Date:

I am grateful for...

I am grateful for...

I am grateful for...

Today I will...

"Gratitude, like faith, is a muscle.

The more you use it, the stronger it grows,
and the more power you have to use it on
your behalf. If you do not practice gratefulness, it's
benefaction will go unnoticed, and your capacity
to draw on its gifts will be diminished. To be
grateful is to find blessings in everyting. This is
the most powerful attitude to adopt, for there are
blessings in everything."

– Alan Cohen

Day: Date:

I am grateful for...

I am grateful for...

I am grateful for...

Today I will...

Day: Date:

I am grateful for...

I am grateful for...

I am grateful for...

Today I will...

Day: Date:

I am grateful for...

I am grateful for...

I am grateful for...

Today I will...

Day: Date:

I am grateful for...

I am grateful for...

I am grateful for...

Today I will...

Day: Date:

I am grateful for...

I am grateful for...

I am grateful for...

Today I will...

Day: Date:

I am grateful for...

I am grateful for...

I am grateful for...

Today I will...

Day: Date:

I am grateful for...

I am grateful for...

I am grateful for...

Today I will...

"There is always something to be thankful for."

Day: Date:

I am grateful for...

I am grateful for...

I am grateful for...

Today I will...

Day: Date:

I am grateful for...

I am grateful for...

I am grateful for...

Today I will...

Day: Date:

I am grateful for...

I am grateful for...

I am grateful for...

Today I will...

Day: Date:

I am grateful for...

I am grateful for...

I am grateful for...

Today I will...

108

Day: Date:

I am grateful for...

I am grateful for...

I am grateful for...

Today I will...

Day: Date:

I am grateful for...

I am grateful for...

I am grateful for...

Today I will...

Day: Date:

I am grateful for...

I am grateful for...

I am grateful for...

Today I will...

"Gratitude can transform common
days into thanksgiving,
turn routine jobs into joy,
and change ordinary opportunities
into blessings."

– *William Arthur Ward*

Day: Date:

I am grateful for...

I am grateful for...

I am grateful for...

Today I will...

Day: Date:

I am grateful for...

I am grateful for...

I am grateful for...

Today I will...

Day: Date:

I am grateful for...

I am grateful for...

I am grateful for...

Today I will...

Day: Date:

I am grateful for...

I am grateful for...

I am grateful for...

Today I will...

116

Day: Date:

I am grateful for...

I am grateful for...

I am grateful for...

Today I will...

Day: Date:

I am grateful for...

I am grateful for...

I am grateful for...

Today I will...

Day: Date:

I am grateful for...

I am grateful for...

I am grateful for...

Today I will...

"Trade your expectation for appreciation and the world changes instantly."

– *Tony Robbins*

Day: Date:

I am grateful for...

I am grateful for...

I am grateful for...

Today I will...

Day: Date:

I am grateful for...

I am grateful for...

I am grateful for...

Today I will...

Day: Date:

I am grateful for...

I am grateful for...

I am grateful for...

Today I will...

Day: Date:

I am grateful for...

I am grateful for...

I am grateful for...

Today I will...

Day: Date:

I am grateful for...

I am grateful for...

I am grateful for...

Today I will...

Day: Date:

I am grateful for...

I am grateful for...

I am grateful for...

Today I will...

Day: Date:

I am grateful for...

I am grateful for...

I am grateful for...

Today I will...

"What are you grateful for today?"

Day: Date:

I am grateful for...

I am grateful for...

I am grateful for...

Today I will...

Day: Date:

I am grateful for...

I am grateful for...

I am grateful for...

Today I will...

Day: Date:

I am grateful for...

I am grateful for...

I am grateful for...

Today I will...

Day: Date:

I am grateful for...

I am grateful for...

I am grateful for...

Today I will...

Day: Date:

I am grateful for...

I am grateful for...

I am grateful for...

Today I will...

Day: Date:

I am grateful for...

I am grateful for...

I am grateful for...

Today I will...

Day: Date:

I am grateful for...

I am grateful for...

I am grateful for...

Today I will...

If you want to find happiness,
find gratitude."

– Steve Maraboli

Day: Date:

I am grateful for...

I am grateful for...

I am grateful for...

Today I will...

Day: Date:

I am grateful for...

I am grateful for...

I am grateful for...

Today I will...

Day: Date:

I am grateful for...

I am grateful for...

I am grateful for...

Today I will...

Day: Date:

I am grateful for...

I am grateful for...

I am grateful for...

Today I will...

140

Day: Date:

I am grateful for...

I am grateful for...

I am grateful for...

Today I will...

Day: Date:

I am grateful for...

I am grateful for...

I am grateful for...

Today I will...

Day: Date:

I am grateful for...

I am grateful for...

I am grateful for...

Today I will...

Gratitude is the best attitude."

Day: Date:

I am grateful for...

I am grateful for...

I am grateful for...

Today I will...

Day: Date:

I am grateful for...

I am grateful for...

I am grateful for...

Today I will...

Day: Date:

I am grateful for...

I am grateful for...

I am grateful for...

Today I will...

Day: Date:

I am grateful for...

I am grateful for...

I am grateful for...

Today I will...

Day: Date:

I am grateful for...

I am grateful for...

I am grateful for...

Today I will...

Day: Date:

I am grateful for...

I am grateful for...

I am grateful for...

Today I will...

150

Day: Date:

I am grateful for...

I am grateful for...

I am grateful for...

Today I will...

"Gratitude is more than an attitude, it is a lifestyle."

– *Jenni Mullinix*

Day: Date:

I am grateful for...

I am grateful for...

I am grateful for...

Today I will...

Day: Date:

I am grateful for...

I am grateful for...

I am grateful for...

Today I will...

Day: Date:

I am grateful for...

I am grateful for...

I am grateful for...

Today I will...

Day: Date:

I am grateful for...

I am grateful for...

I am grateful for...

Today I will...

Day: Date:

I am grateful for...

I am grateful for...

I am grateful for...

Today I will...

Gratitude helps you to grow and expand;
gratitude brings joy and laughter into
your life and into the lives of
all those around you."

– Eileen Caddy

Day: Date:

I am grateful for...

I am grateful for...

I am grateful for...

Today I will...

Day: Date:

I am grateful for...

I am grateful for...

I am grateful for...

Today I will...

Day: Date:

I am grateful for...

I am grateful for...

I am grateful for...

Today I will...

Day: Date:

I am grateful for...

I am grateful for...

I am grateful for...

Today I will...

162

Day: Date:

I am grateful for...

I am grateful for...

I am grateful for...

Today I will...

Day: Date:

I am grateful for...

I am grateful for...

I am grateful for...

Today I will...

"Gratitude is the secret drug. It is the gateway drug to the motivation drug."

– *Gary Vaynerchuk*

Day: Date:

I am grateful for...

I am grateful for...

I am grateful for...

Today I will...

Day: Date:

I am grateful for...

I am grateful for...

I am grateful for...

Today I will...

Day: Date:

I am grateful for...

I am grateful for...

I am grateful for...

Today I will...

Day: Date:

I am grateful for...

I am grateful for...

I am grateful for...

Today I will...

Day: Date:

I am grateful for...

I am grateful for...

I am grateful for...

Today I will...

Day: Date:

I am grateful for...

I am grateful for...

I am grateful for...

Today I will...

As we express our gratitude,

we must never forget that

the highest appreciation is

not to utter words, but

to live by them."

– John F. Kennedy

Day: Date:

I am grateful for...

I am grateful for...

I am grateful for...

Today I will...

Day: Date:

I am grateful for...

I am grateful for...

I am grateful for...

Today I will...

Day: Date:

I am grateful for...

I am grateful for...

I am grateful for...

Today I will...

Day: Date:

I am grateful for...

I am grateful for...

I am grateful for...

Today I will...

Day: Date:

I am grateful for...

I am grateful for...

I am grateful for...

Today I will...

Day: Date:

I am grateful for...

I am grateful for...

I am grateful for...

Today I will...

"When you are grateful
fear disappears and
abundance appears."

– Tony Robbins

Day: Date:

I am grateful for...

I am grateful for...

I am grateful for...

Today I will...

Day: Date:

I am grateful for...

I am grateful for...

I am grateful for...

Today I will...

Day: Date:

I am grateful for...

I am grateful for...

I am grateful for...

Today I will...

Day: Date:

I am grateful for...

I am grateful for...

I am grateful for...

Today I will...

Day: Date:

I am grateful for...

I am grateful for...

I am grateful for...

Today I will...

184

Day: Date:

I am grateful for...

I am grateful for...

I am grateful for...

Today I will...

W hen you look at life
through eye of gratitude,
the world becomes a
magical and amazing place."

– Paula Tooths

Day: Date:

I am grateful for...

I am grateful for...

I am grateful for...

Today I will...

Day: Date:

I am grateful for...

I am grateful for...

I am grateful for...

Today I will...

Day: Date:

I am grateful for...

I am grateful for...

I am grateful for...

Today I will...

Day: Date:

I am grateful for...

I am grateful for...

I am grateful for...

Today I will...

Day: Date:

I am grateful for...

I am grateful for...

I am grateful for...

Today I will...

Day: Date:

I am grateful for...

I am grateful for...

I am grateful for...

Today I will...

Day: Date:

I am grateful for...

I am grateful for...

I am grateful for...

Today I will...